Three Houses

Phaidon Press Limited
Regent's Wharf
All Saints Street
London N1 9PA

Phaidon Press, Inc
180 Varick Street
New York, NY 10014

www.phaidon.com

First published 1993
Reprinted 1994, 1996
This edition first published 2002
Reprinted 2002
© 1993, 2002 Phaidon Press Limited
Photographs © 1993 Anthony
Browell, except where stated to the
contrary

ISBN 0 7148 4219 2

Printed in Hong Kong

Text illustrations are reproduced
with the kind permission of:
The Architectural Press (1, 5 and
37); Adrian Boddy (13, 21 and 26);
Max Dupain (23, 24, 28, 29 and
31); Eric Sierins (38, 43 and 44) and
Glenn Murcutt (41, 42 and 48).

Three Houses
Glenn Murcutt

E M Farrelly
ARCHITECTURE IN DETAIL

1

Glenn Murcutt is now Australia's most celebrated architect,[1] and unlike most of his very few peers atop the Australian tree he has got there without ever having built abroad. Surprisingly little, perhaps in consequence, has been written about him; and surprisingly little of that makes any attempt at serious analysis, tending instead to accept at face value the standard, populist myth which bills the Murcutt *oeuvre* as 'a distinctive Australian architecture – an amazing fusion of bush vernacular and minimalist Modernism'.[2]

This sounds unexceptionable, but contrary impulses are at work. There is on the one hand a desire to present Murcutt as romantic primitivist and on the other, the obvious fact of a Miesian inheritance and a minimalist, rationalist mind-set.

The former impulse, its emphasis varying according to context, surfaces within Australia as a generalized perception of Murcutt as a kind of bush Wordsworth, responding with minute caress to every pock and ant hill of the landscape; 'mystic poet and spiritual guardian of Australian architectural values, a contemporary national romantic who nevertheless transcends the narrow confines of parochialism'.[3] Abroad it appears, more crudely, in such headlines as 'Essence of the Outback',[4] 'Outback Warrior'[5] and even 'Outback Fashion'[6]. But the rustic theory quickly loses plausibility in the face of the uncompromising plan discipline, refined steel detailing, and remarkable formal consistency (all anti-aesthetic protestations notwithstanding), which manifest a mind which is not only supremely rational – more Foster than Goff or even Wright, **1** – but unabashedly Rationalist in its approach.[7]

So, impasse. The obvious solution is to go for the kind of both-and assessment which has become standard since post-Modernism made a virtue of ambiguity, enabling the myth to be propagated as a dialectical unity of opposites. This is precisely the approach taken, for instance, by the committee for the 1992 Alvar Aalto Award,[8] whose citation read, in part: 'Glenn Murcutt's work is a reassuring and inspiring example of the capacity of contemporary architecture to respond to new ecological, social, technological challenges. His architecture is a convincing synthesis of regional character, climate-conditioned solutions, technological rationality and unconstrained visual expression.

'In his designs, Murcutt fuses ingredients of modernity and elements of an indigenous rural tradition to create structures that appear self-evident and innovative, idiosyncratic and traditional, locally-rooted and universal at the same time. His buildings are a poetic interaction between nature, landscape and culture.

'Murcutt has been among the pioneers in developing a new ecologically-responsive and socially-responsible architecture as a valid alternative to the prodigality of the consumer society. Murcutt's series of small, mostly rural and suburban houses represents a gradual and logical development of building types and economical construction methods that exhibit the ethical and poetic value of concentration and restraint'.

It is tempting. But such dialectical facility demands scrutiny. To what extent does the warm inclusive glow obscure, rather than enlighten? How far does Murcutt's work actually embrace social challenge, regional character or indigenous rural tradition? Is it possible to be as both-and as the citation suggests – both particular and universal, for instance – without going altogether out of focus?

For these buildings are nothing if not focused. They are in addition, from an architectonic point of view, inspirationally, forbiddingly simple. Rationalizing function, eschewing decoration and disciplining space to the point of regimentation, Murcutt's buildings are, at that level, ruthlessly Modern. Calvinist even.

But any more sustained analysis of their spatial ordering, formal semantics or generative ideas, not to mention their seductive imagery, reveals much greater complexity – and, yes, contradiction: buildings which are Romantic and Classical, Rationalist and regionalist, Modern and post-Modern by turns. Normally, after Venturi, such contradictions are themselves taken as definitive shibboleths of the post-Modern faith, yet most of Murcutt's colleagues, including some of the closest and most perceptive, persist in regarding him unequivocally as a card-carrying Modernist.

Perhaps, one might argue, it doesn't matter. Perhaps the very attempt at classification is itself misguided, a futile exercise in the positivistic delusion that existence is at root intelligible. But, manipulate the problem how you will, the buildings emit and are formed by ideas whose basic incompatibility is irreducible, however it may be disguised. In most hands contradictions of this kind end merely in miasmic compromise; Murcutt is one of the very few whose work, contrariwise, is enriched by such tangibly incompatible presences. Why is this so? What is the special skill or quality that can transform

a potential weakness of this kind into a positive strength?

The answer, in a word, is discipline. It is discipline – in practice, in methodology, in design – that gives his buildings their unnerving, irresistible clarity, and the capacity to carry conflicting messages without cacophony. Murcutt steadfastly eschews the big building, the big practice and what he disparagingly calls 'the commercial reality' – though he takes no umbrage at the normal design constraints of economic exigency. He does things the way he believes they should be done, or not at all. He rails against local authorities ('they are so often stupid, absolutely stupid, and unreasonable'[9]) and defends design against the everyday encroachments of normal urban mediocrity: 'We're in a really low-brow period. I'm not going to be part of that. I'm not going to compromise… I'd like to go to the grave without any of that. That's the reality for me. I've got a conscience'. And explaining his reluctance to work in the city, for instance, Murcutt says, 'all too frequently the established land pattern hinders design'.[10] Such views, common enough during the Modernist era, are comparatively unusual now, when most

2

3

4

5

thinking architects (and quite a few besides) have hung their hat on urban design, with all (or at least some of) the compromise and self-effacement that that inevitably entails. Few these days would defend, much less shape their lives, to the sanctity and purity of the design act.

Should sentiments like these be taken as hubristic rarefication – or as dedicated humility? How easily do they sit in fact with stances of environmental and client responsiveness – stances which generically claim sensitivity to factors that might themselves be regarded similarly as hindrances to 'design'? How precisely does any of this bear on a body of work which comprises in the main buildings whose intra-familial connections are more conspicuous by far than any such relatedness to specific site or programme? What are we to make of the more or less familiar charge that Murcutt repeatedly designs the same building? And how does he contrive to resolve the obvious metaphysical contradictions into buildings which not only cohere but positively radiate unity?

Taking three of Murcutt's most iconic houses, I will investigate some of these questions; testing the myth against the buildings, and the buildings against the myth, in pursuit of the still unresolved question 'where *is* Murcutt coming from?'.[11]

Thoreau

Was Thoreau really as central to Murcutt's intellectual development as has been suggested?[12] Yes, says Murcutt, launching unhesitatingly into rhythmic recital: 'the mass of men lead lives of quiet desperation. What is called resignation is confirmed desperation'[13] and 'most men appear never to have considered what a house is… [except] they think that they must have such a one as their neighbours have'.[14] Thoreau's influence reverberates throughout not only Murcutt's conversation, but his work. Explaining his predilection for the casual entrance, as in the Ball-Eastaway house for instance, Murcutt paraphrases Thoreau: 'three most important things; first, simplicity; second, simplicity; third, simplicity'.[15]

Try as one might, the childhood is unavoidable. Murcutt's upbringing – like that of his own children, as it happens – was strongly patriarchal, and even now in Glenn's conversational narrative his father is constantly, charismatically present. (His mother, by contrast, who came from a gentle, cultivated family and was grand-niece of John Cowper Powys, appears seldom, although her substantial contribution to the man and his work is clearly evident.)

Sydney Arthur (Sam) Murcutt, born 1899, was a truly extraordinary man. Leaving the home of his mathematician/musician father at the age of eleven he cycled 600km from Sydney to Bourke, to become a shearer, boxer, and later gold-miner, philosopher, boat-builder, inventor, timber-miller, naturalist, disciplinarian, musician, adventurer and tireless designer and builder of houses. In 1919 he went to live in New Guinea. The story is that on a walking expedition between Port Moresby[16] and Lae, Sam Murcutt, who alone survived the mountainous trek, carried with him a first edition of Freud and the journals of Henry David Thoreau. This then became a profound osmotic influence on his life and the lives of his children. Glenn only latterly recognized the full extent of Thoreau's intellectual and spiritual influence on the family, but has felt no need to reject it, saying simply 'that was how I was raised'.

Thoreau's central ideas were not original but they were vividly expressed, namely that the individual conscience was a higher authority than law, that it must be followed regardless of the cost, that life was too valuable to be wasted earning a living, that the world of trees and streams was good, the world of streets and crowds bad; that the individual is the source and mainstay of civilization; that governments and mass actions are not to be trusted, and that the practice of economy and simplicity, in life as much as in aesthetic endeavours, was almost a moral duty.

Sam Murcutt lived very much according to this creed. Was Thoreau a role model for him? 'He was certainly quoted enough for me to believe it', says Murcutt, adding that Thoreau's obsessive economizing was 'my father to a T' – providing an outlet for his inventor's determination to 'find the best solution' with the means available.

All of this is clearly present too in the Murcutt *oeuvre*: the insistence on simplicity; the distrust of government and whole-hearted belief in the individual; the unshakeable sense of connectedness with nature;[17] the embrace of artifice in the service of that relationship, but almost complete disdain of aesthetics, composition and the conventions of the artificial world; the problem-solving approach to architecture and unswerving commitment to discovering[18] the most elegant solution; the determination to work in a manner which he finds philosophically palatable.

Murcutt recalls his father's view of architects as 'dishonest brokers of a noble profession'[19] and Thoreau's 'description of the honest house; that the whole house was exposed before you, that there was nothing hidden, that it was an honest expression of a human's life, in very simple terms… That's what I call legibility'.

This link between the primitive and the modern is hardly unfamiliar, having been the source of much of Modernism's moral authority, as well as its romantic appeal. But whereas for Modernists in the tradition of Viollet le Duc, for instance, the commitment to 'honesty' was primarily structural, in Murcutt's terms it implies honesty – openness – in plan, **6**. Thoreau reinforces this: 'I sometimes dream of … a house whose inside is as open and manifest as a bird's nest … where to be a guest is to be presented with the freedom of the house, and not carefully excluded from seven-eighths of it, shut up in a particular cell…'.[20]

This no doubt explains to a large degree the magnetic appeal of Modernism both to Sam Murcutt and to his eldest son. Murcutt senior subscribed to 'all the architectural journals you could possibly get, pre-war and post-war', and raised his children on modern architecture. 'My father imbued my psyche with it', says Murcutt. 'Mies, Gordon Drake, the Philip Johnson house, the Eames house, **5**,

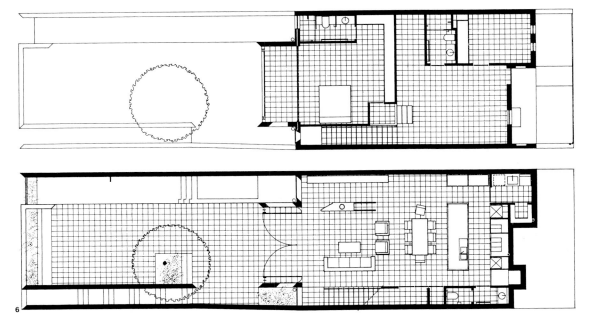

6

and Frank Lloyd Wright more than anybody. I knew all of Frank Lloyd Wright's work by the time I was 14 or 15', **1**.

Wright's influence, clearly evidenced in Murcutt's student work, **7**, is undetectable in the buildings. But the legibility principle remains for Murcutt an article of faith. No receding layers for him, no gradual introductions, no games of concealment and discovery. In a Murcutt house you're either in, or you're out – but once you're in, it's all there for you. 'Once you've punctured the private world, you are no longer a guest. You are really part of that private world.'

Private and public
And the private world, for Murcutt, is the world that matters. 'I hate the public realm', he says – meaning, really, that he regrets the necessity for public speaking that recognition seems to bring, and at the age of 57 predicts for himself an increasingly eremitic later life, like his father's. The public realm in a broader, non-personal sense seems not to figure at all. Privacy on the other hand is something he actively seeks – anonymity for himself, and a 'withdrawn quality' for his houses.

'I like my buildings so that you could almost walk past them and not know they're there', he says, claiming pleasure in the fact that people have done precisely this. (The work of Barragán, **8**, and Chareau's Maison

de Verre[21] – private to the point of self-effacement – he counts amongst his most formative influences.) Privacy has for so long been the predominant value of Murcutt's life and work that even to regard it as an issue, much less question it, seems to surprise him. 'What is a front?', he asks, insouciant. 'The sides, the rear … isn't the whole of a building public?'

One of the corollaries of all this, in terms of architecture, is a typically modern attitude to streets, to cities and to the business of entry. Here the legibility principle emphatically does not apply: the buildings, like the man, resolutely resist any impulse to don a public face. Especially in rural settings, Murcutt explains, the 'psychological vulnerability' of remoteness makes it desirable to 'put the arrivee at a disadvantage': the Kempsey and Bingie Point houses effect this both by giving the house visual command of the approach road, and by concealing the 'front' door, **9**, **10**. But the suburban houses too are markedly unforthcoming. Even on those rare occasions where the house is forced by circumstance (usually the size of the site) to recognize the street[22] there is no attempt at frontality, no elaboration of the entry ritual, no overt gesture of welcome.

This is not to say that the typical Murcutt entrance is unpleasant or un-thought through: on the contrary, the entrances are characteristically elegant, well-lit, skilfully modulated spaces – on the inside. Nor is Murcutt unaware of the issue. He recounts with glee the story of Frank Lloyd Wright's appearance at a party at the Philip Johnson house; Wright circled the building several times, tapping on the glass to demonstrate his inability to find the door.

But from without the Murcutt entrance remains emphatically understated. Why?

In part, of course, it may be accounted for by natural good taste. 'The last thing I want', says Murcutt, 'is for my buildings to be screamingly yelling out saying here I am.' But legibility needn't imply loudness. There has to be more to it. The clue, once again, lies in childhood patterns – and the uncanny ease with which so idiosyncratic an upbringing dovetailed into international Modernism.

Murcutt recalls the way in which, for instance, once a year, he and his four siblings would scoop the school swimming prizes, winning almost everything, to the point of embarrassment. No-one at school knew about the private, back-yard training programme, devised by their father, who turned them into champion sprinters and water-polo players by devoting their leisure hours to swimming on the end of a restraining rubber band. The same was true of 'our piano'; to the outside world the distinctions seemed to come from nowhere. 'And I'm still doing it', he says. 'I've only just realized. I'm here working by myself, quietly, nobody knows what I'm doing. Then I used to come out, go to the awards, win them, go away … it's no different.' It's a fact. All but one of the Murcutt buildings entered in the Institute awards over the years has been premiated. But Murcutt sounds almost ashamed.

These days he no longer enters awards of course,[23] but the pattern remains, both in lifestyle and in architecture. Take for instance the determination to work alone; no partners, no assistant, no secretary. Why? 'I value my privacy', replies Murcutt. But it is important to recognize this as an architectural choice, as much as a personal one; a choice which is steadfastly maintained against lengthening queues of clients and a pace of life, these days, that makes even the normal professional fray look relaxed.

Such a choice is sustainable only through the application of the kind of rigorous and intensive discipline for which Murcutt is known and admired amongst his peers, and which is justified, in his estimation, only because it enables him to retain (as far as is humanly possible) complete control of the building and process, a direct relationship with the client and an intimate hands-on knowledge of the site. His refusal to delegate even at the most trivial level leaves clients waiting commonly for years before reaching even butter paper stage; but also allows him, crucially, to produce the kinds of buildings for which more than enough people are more than happy to wait.

The time he takes is Murcutt's primary luxury. In the early days of his success he bought property; these days, the investment is all in time – time to do the jobs that he wants to do, in the way he thinks they should be done. Time to get it right.

Ironically, however, although commitment of this kind *is* admired, it also generates, precisely because it limits him to working on a domestic scale,[24] the most frequent criticism of Glenn Murcutt, architect – namely the old gibe about villas for the élite and avoidance of the hard urban issues.

On the class question Murcutt becomes justifiably defensive, pointing out that many of his houses are not expensive, comparatively, having cost as little as A$40,000;[25] that he is

9

10

13

14

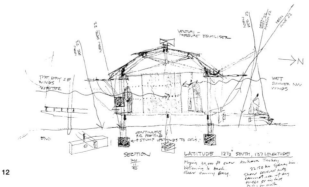

11

12

currently working on a (very elegant) house for an Aboriginal woman in East Arnhemland which, if used as he intends as a prototype, will constitute a radical and welcome change from the concrete bunkers that are still standard issue in the area, **11**, **12**; and that he regularly sends out, to other architects who ask, details of for instance, his highly refined sun-screening systems that 'work with the geometry of the planet'.

'I don't look at patents as something relevant to the 21st century … People have got to be able to use the things that one develops', he says, adding, 'if I can find a way of dealing appropriately with this country – and I'm not saying I have – but if I've done that, then its a bloody sight more than most people do in their lifetime… .'

With regard to the city, however, Murcutt is unabashed. For him the moral imperative points to withdrawal, not engagement, especially in a city like Sydney 'where greed is the driving force'. He greatly admires Harry Seidler, who has worked primarily in the city, saying, 'he's done a real Haussman', but adds, 'you couldn't get away with doing a Haussman any longer'.[26] 'I am not rejecting urbanization', he says.[27] But fundamentally anti-urban attitudes reappear constantly, with various emphases. Does he still reject working in the city? 'Sure. Its so boring … dealing with the mainstream you're dealing with

developers. And at the bottom of the mainstream lies mediocrity … they're the rapists of our city.' Big projects? 'I hate the idea. Show me one in Sydney that contributes to anybody's daily existence … all these bloody regulations try to prevent it going wrong, and only make it worse.' And, 'I am not interested in designing large-scale works. Our building regulations prescribe mediocrity and our councils administer and police such conservatism'.

He laments 'the wholesale slaughter of our city', by developers, but sees this process as complete, describing Sydney city centre as 'a whole gaggle of rubbish … junk and rubbish', **13**. So what of urban design? Murcutt is capable of becoming quite excited about city design – the notion for instance of a city without air-conditioning, maximizing winter sunlight and ventilation (as he speaks he sketches the triangular design profiles so generated) but says, 'it's too late for Sydney. If you had Sydney to start with…'. Such a *tabula rasa* approach is of course inimical to current urban design theory – but wholly in keeping with the Murcutt emphasis on individuation. 'I believe the man is more a man by being an individual rather than a committee meeting.'[28] 'I believe in the individual. All great things have come from the individual.'

Again the echoes of Thoreau are unmistakeable. 'There will never be a free and enlightened state until the state comes to recognize the individual as a higher and independent power, from which all its own power and authority are derived, and treats him accordingly.'[29] It is scarcely surprising therefore that the detached rural or suburban house should represent for Murcutt this ideal of design freedom.

'Domestic-scale work offers me a chance to challenge the ordinances. It permits me to conceptualize and build many more ideas than is possible in one large project. The design of individual houses represents, therefore, a platform for exploring solutions to specific problems. I especially enjoy working outside the confines of the city. In the countryside I am able to draw more fully on the special character of the land'[30], **14**.

Nature: extension of self or essential other?

What, then, aside from its part as not-city, is the role of Nature in Murcutt's work? That Murcutt's is pre-eminently 'an architecture of place' seems to be unanimous amongst the commentators. The work is programme-specific, climate-specific, culture-specific and, above all, site-specific;[31] environmentally-sensitive and almost mystically in tune with the landscape – or so runs the

myth. Murcutt himself stresses the importance of 'wind patterns, materials, climate and spaces, and, *most important of all, the characteristics of the site*'.[32] Articles tend to dwell poetically on the 'sense of place' created by these buildings and yet, as even Murcutt's own aphorism about 'touching the land lightly'[33] suggests, the relationship between the buildings and what is said about them warrants further examination.

Formally, at least, as objects, the houses are related more obviously to each other than to the peculiarities of place. This suggests Rationalism, not romanticism; a designer interested in universals, not specifics; absolutes, not contingents. Is this contradiction real? How can it be resolved? Where does truth lie?

Murcutt himself denies any complicity in the myth-making, regarding that as an occupation for others. But an obsession with 'place' is something he cannot, and would not, deny. In conversation he returns to it again and again; pressed on almost any characteristic of almost any building – be it roof form, spatial ordering, materials, construction, or attitudes to the public realm – Murcutt will proffer some

aspect of place as primary determinant. Only the plan remains consciously tied to cultural precedent, **15**, **16**.

'Place' for Murcutt includes both site and climate – and while 'site' itself might be expected to cover some aesthetic response to topography, Murcutt does his best to deny aesthetic sensibility of any kind. Everything is explained in terms of pragmatics – water tables, wind patterns, sun angles, soil types, wildlife, rainfall, humidity, material and economic exigency. Not to mention programme. But there is one principle – responsible, arguably, for much of these houses' profound international appeal – which informs every house, and every detail, and which is wholly aesthetic in its import. It is to do with what Murcutt calls 'confronting'.

Murcutt's own oft-used metaphor for the siting process runs thus: 'If I throw a brick into the waves, after two hours the sand and the sea will have operated in such a way to structure channels and contours around the brick, merging it with the beach. After five hours the brick will have found its proper position or "place". I'm interested in finding that "place" for my houses'.[34] It would be a mistake, though, to read any formal import

15

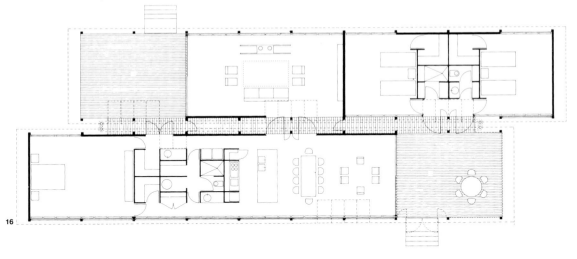

16

17 The Magney house's winged roof emulates the lightness – not the form – of living under canvas. The refinement and lift of the edges was all important to Murcutt.
18 The Magney house extends no more than a tiny mat into its austere, inhospitable landscape.
19 The Ball-Eastaway house too is absolutely separate from its landscape – and absolutely interwoven: 'harmony', says Murcutt, 'is about disparateness'.

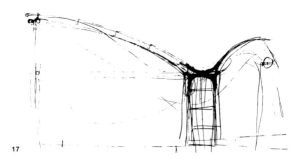

17

18

19

into the metaphor. The fact is that the last thing these houses do is snuggle in. Standing warily tip-toed on truncated piloti, eschewing the traditional 'feathering' forms of eaves and verandah, assuming an emphatically artificial geometry and underlining precision in every detail, they consciously dissociate themselves from the natural world. Nor are the traditional tools of landscape architecture employed. The Kempsey house had a pergola, not designed by Murcutt, and which he has since removed; few of the others extend more than a tiny paved mat by way of claim on the landscape. No fence, no wall, no garden. True to maxim, they touch the land lightly.

Doesn't this contradict the harmonizing principle suggested by the metaphor? 'Not at all', says Murcutt. 'Harmony is about disparateness, about disparate sounds which when put together make a pleasing whole… not monotony, not sameness. I am actually harmonizing by confronting, in a sense.'

There are one or two exceptions, one or two formal echoes of the landscape. The Bingie Point house for instance parallels its eaves, north and south, to the slope of the hill, **17**, **18**; the walls in the Ball-Eastaway house are aligned like iron filings with the linearity of the rock formations beneath, **19**. But on the whole the moored-ship quality is consciously sought. Murcutt talks about the beauty of contrasts – new and old, smooth and rough etc. Both-and. 'If both hold their integrity, each will tell about the other. One clarifies the order of the other. I am interested in that.'

For 'interested in' read something like 'obsessed by'. Here, formally, Nature's role is that of the essential Other, defining and identifying through contrast.

'To hide like an ant in the landscape', says Murcutt, in another favourite metaphor,[35] 'tells me nothing about the Other … I think that that difference is very important. Not for difference's sake; difference must come out of an under-standing of scale, of material, of structure, of light, of shade, of wind, of smells, of sun, of the verandah, the change from outside to inside, the structure of the landscape… .' The litany continues.

The fact is that the form and function of these houses are marching in opposite directions. Formally they stand aloof. More Villa Rotonda than Villa Mairea they express – indeed, proclaim – humanity's separateness from and dominance over Nature. The intimacy, the intricate inter-weaving of house and nature happens at the other, physiological level, the level of the myriad unseen parameters: 'we've got to keep working with the invisible. The things we don't know. The discovery…'. The forms are universal, Rationalist: their working, however, is particular, empirical and contingent.

This does nothing to weaken the nature–artifice relationship, of course. Indeed one might argue that such a relationship is immeasurably strengthened by a commitment to developing roofs, screening systems and so on that work so closely with the patterns of sun, wind and water. But it does lead to a curious irony. Because the intimacy of the house–nature relationship is thus largely invisible, and unphotographable, it has played only a small part in the making of the Murcutt myth. But the expectation of regionalism remains, attaching an only partially convincing 'Australian' tag to these overtly rationalist icons, and giving rise to all sorts of wishful misapprehensions to do with woolsheds, barns and humpys, **20**, **21**.[36]

The Australianness question

Rightly or wrongly, though, Murcutt has come to be regarded both at home and abroad as pre-eminently an Australian architect – in many ways *the* Australian architect. At first this might seem to sit very easily with the site-responsiveness principle. But does it, in fact?

Murcutt points out that in Australia, a country the size of Europe, each site is different; even within New South Wales his sites vary from the red desert of Broken Hill to the swampy sub-tropics of Kempsey[37] and the dry rocky bushland of Glenorie. No consistent 'Australianness' could be expected to derive that way. Murcutt's answer is that his principles are universal, but because they are principles about responsiveness to place, the results of their application – the buildings – are particular. 'I am trying to respond to where I am', he says, pointing out that if he were living in America, he would be responding, from the same principles, to that place – and that the reason he doesn't work abroad, as he has been invited to do,[38] is due less to undying patriotism than to a simple recognition of the fact that the subtleties of other cultures cannot be properly grasped within a few weeks. 'I'm interested in more than gestures', he says.

So far so plausible. But the fact remains that while the buildings may be environmentally particular, their formal nature springs from a patently Rationalist base; and it is their formal qualities that have earned them their reputation as iconic Australians. Critics have spoken of woolsheds and shearing sheds – the formal symmetry, the tin, the temporary look.[39]

Perhaps the Australianness is in the perception, not the act. Perhaps Murcutt's Australianness is simply what the audience has wanted to see. The world – including Australia itself – imagines Australia as a rude, rural, honourable land, infinitely open, somewhere between Ayers Rock and the sea. Even now Murcutt's more solid and centred urban houses are much less widely published than the open-ended shed icons, enveloped in vastness, which brought him to fame.

Murcutt had received awards and recognition before, but the Marie Short house (1974–75), **22**, **25**, and the Mt Irvine houses (1977–80), **23**, **24**, emerged towards the end of the Whitlam years, when the entire country seemed to be agitating about what it meant, culturally, to be Australian. With their magical settings and irresistible formal imageability, these houses sprang into popular consciousness as having somehow answered the question; as having given form to Australianness. 'The houses most immediately impress … with a sense of place', reads the Institute of Architects' awards blurb for 1981.[40] 'Both houses are built above the ground … in the manner of barns or woolsheds. The simple forms of

20 A typical communal bark shelter, Arnhemland.

21 Uluru (or Ayers Rock) – the look of Australia: but is being Australian the same as looking Australian?

22 Marie Short house interior: woodsy materials, refinement of thought and detail.

23 Carruthers house, Mt Irvine, NSW (1978–80) was one of the first of two houses that first brought Glenn Murcutt into public consciousness around 1980; deceptively primitive form plus environmental sophistication equals seductive elegance.

22

23

26

24

25

these earlier building types are further evoked
by the forms of the houses themselves.
Both exploit that humble but ubiquitous
material, corrugated galvanized iron… .'

Craig McGregor, documenting in 1985 what
he described as a peculiarly Australian return
to 'a much more direct, instinctual,
accommodating approach to the problem
of living on the land' saw Murcutt's work in
particular as part of a generalized architectural
re-enactment of white settlement, emphasized
by the 'application of traditional materials
(galvanized iron) and shapes (farmhouse
rooflines) to Modernist principles…'.[41]

But are the formal simplicity, the elegant
plans and untramelled settings, the
corrugated iron and the intimations of
innocence sufficient qualification?

Innocence, arguably, is a part of what
Australia, in the world's eyes, stands for.
Symbol of infinite distance, Australia
symbolizes too, however spuriously, a sort
of lost Eden, and these so-elegant sheds,
slender but self-possessed, simple (but hardly
unsophisticated), poised but (beyond the
louvred skin) undefended in their landscape,
seem to represent, to jaded post-Modern
sensibilities, a return to a pastoral serenity. But
how Australian are they? Perhaps the
very alacrity with which these impermanent
'space-ships' have been acclaimed as
national icons itself says something about
the culture–nature relationship in Australia?

In the end of course the questions
become meaningless. But it is worth noting
that most of the distinguishing
characteristics of the work – excepting
perhaps the corrugated iron – are more
convincingly connected to International
Modernism than to any distinctively
Australian culture.

Murcutt has learned much from Australia,
and Australians, but the principles, to
reiterate, are universal. The forms, rather
than being 'applied' (in McGregor's phrase)
to Modernist principles, are drawn by them
from the site conditions. Murcutt denies
outright being consciously 'Australian' in his
work; 'if by some chance people think my
work is Australian,' he says, 'so be it, but
I'm not setting out to do it'.[42]

He admits to having 'always been
interested in the shearing shed'[43], **26**, but
rejects out of hand the notion that the
vernacular provides any sort of formal
model for his houses. 'That's very superficial isn't it. The reality is that the woolshed
came out of a particular function, which has
its own integrity, and one doesn't design
buildings to be woolsheds… If people like to
structure myths, that's up to them. I'm
certainly interested in the seat-of-the-pants
directness of vernacular architecture. I like
legibility. Woolsheds have legibility. And
there are overlaps. But the construction
technique [of the Kempsey house] has

nothing whatsoever to do with the
woolshed. And nothing to do with the form
of it either. Nothing to do with the form.'

As far as Aboriginal connections are
concerned, Murcutt allows himself the
occasional simile – likening the oblique
entrance to the Ball-Eastaway house, **27**,
for instance, to the conscious humility
of traditional Aboriginal entry to a spirit-
occupied cave. The Ball-Eastaway house
is by no means an Aboriginal house – but
the landscape, he says 'is their landscape'.

On the whole, however, Murcutt lays 'no
claim whatsoever' to having been
influenced by Aboriginality, either in form or
in 'touching the land lightly'. He further
concedes with chagrin that until 1987 he
'thought there was no Aboriginal
architecture'.[44] Indeed his discovery of the
attitudinal similarities between his work and
Aboriginal houses initially made him feel
depressingly out-aced, he says, although
these same similarities are now a source of
'great confidence and joy'.

There is nevertheless a sense of
Australianness, real or illusory, about
Murcutt's houses. Arguably he has taken
the principles of international Modernism,
and flavoured them with Australia, simply
through operating them, carefully, in Australia
– much as the Burlington/Kent collaboration
flavoured Palladianism with Englishness.
Whether a comparable 'school' of Murcutt

27

will develop remains to be seen. Already of course he has imitators – and not only in Australia – but these on the whole operate strictly through formal and architectonic mimicry, rather than the kind of careful reapplication of principle which a proper understanding of Murcutt would imply.

Is Murcutt a Modernist?
This question, for all its imprecision, has to be asked – underlying as it does all other questions about environmental, contextual and cultural responsiveness. And on the face of it the answer must be yes, surely. Not only does Murcutt eschew decoration and deny so much as a flicker of aesthetic or compositional concern, but he naturally evinces that quasi-theological approach to architecture that gave Modernism so much of its impetus. Even his speech falls easily into the rhythmic cadences of the soapbox, and the buildings too are distinguished by the kind of confidence that comes from unshakeable belief first, then thought. Not that Murcutt is opposed to reason. Far from it. Every proposal is subjected to an almost Popperian testing process, first against known facts, and finally in the laboratory. 'I actually set off in feeling. It's not just

guesswork. It's intuition, understanding. What I feel is right. But the heavy hammer of testing comes pretty fast, and it knocks feeling sideways, a lot. What I'm left with still has the feelings, but I know that when I'm questioned it will still stand up.' What doesn't perform – on all fronts – doesn't survive. There can be no conflict between the poetic and rational requirements of site or programme, because the two are interdependent, 'you can't separate them actually. I don't allow the romantic to be separated from the rational'.

Everything is explained in terms of function; roof form, window detail, plan arrangement. Describing the large steel doors in the Magney house (1991) he says, 'It's nothing to do with composition … I never use Corb's modulor, I never use the golden mean. I look at what is sensible, what is reasonable … sitting height, standing height, structural necessity…'. Perhaps he would subscribe more happily to Aalto's 1mm module – but like any successful architect Murcutt is adept at finding reasons for what he does.

There is the occasional glimpse of Murcutt the composer; in the same breath he will stress the importance of the continuity of the ceiling plane, and of the 'wonderful quality

of freedom' that comes of articulating the wall, door and roof structures separately. And of his use of a flat roof on the Laurie Short house (1972–73) he confesses, 'in those days I felt very strongly about the horizontal line in the landscape…'[45], **28–31**. But generally he sees compositional precepts as simply another straitjacket, made to be shrugged off.

All the Modernist hallmarks are there: the simplicity, the economy, the discipline, the open plan, the joy in separating skin from bone, the moral fervour and the absolute seriousness about architecture as an enterprise. But Modernism too he regards as unacceptably dogmatic. Chareau's Maison de Verre, he says, opened his eyes to this, showing him suddenly that 'there was a poetry to Modernism, an absolute freedom … It unlocked for me the whole notion of discovery, because it was a Modern building, but it was open-ended, it had no dogma'.

But why Chareau, whose connections with Murcutt could scarcely be less apparent? 'It's very inventive', he says, 'the house is full of invention'[46], citing a door handle designed especially for the dignity and convenience of the obstetrician who was required by custom to open the door for his pregnant clients.

28–30 Laurie Short house, Terrey Hills, NSW (1972–73); echoes of Mies are unmistakable, but deceptive. Neither plan nor form ever quite takes its hands off the wheel. As an organism however the house is well proven, having protected several 44-gallon drums of petrol and the owner, from a major bushfire. All survived unscathed: 'these things work', says Murcutt.
31 Laurie Short house, Terrey Hills: 'in those days I felt very strongly about the horizontal line in the landscape…'.

28

29

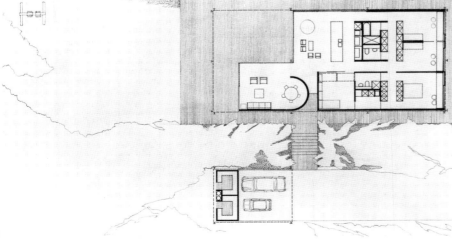

31

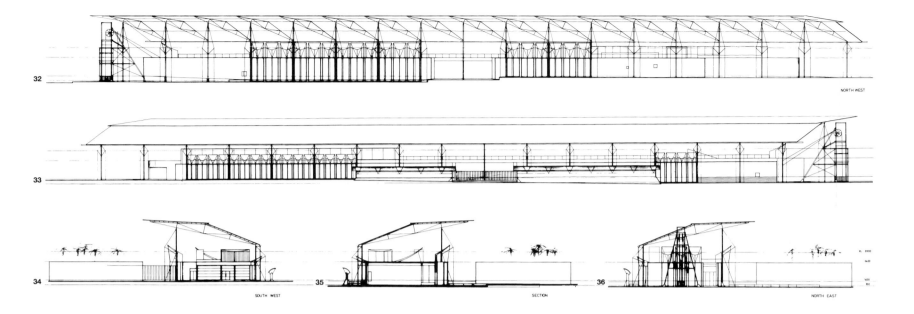

32
NORTH WEST

33

34 SOUTH WEST 35 SECTION 36 NORTH EAST

32–36 Silver City Mining Museum, Broken Hill, NSW (1989) showing *malqafs* (wind scoops): experts' opinions differ as to whether the hot dry wind of the desert would be beneficial.

37 Mies van der Rohe, the steps of Farnsworth House (1946).
38 Magney House, Paddington. Murcutt has used the Mies steps to bridge not inside and out, but old and new.

37

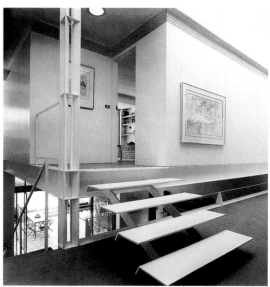

38

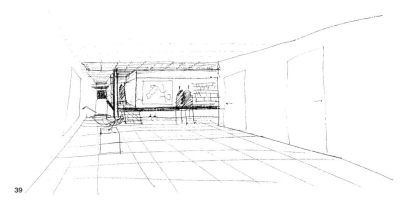

39 Sketch of the ante-room to Magney house.
40 The Ball-Eastaway house: pared ends and edges emphasize its linearity.
41, 42 The courtyard to the Ken Done house, Mosman, NSW (1991): a homage to Barragán? and the entrance, a typical Murcutt railway-carriage of a space heads straight out to sea.

You might see this as simply a more minute responsiveness to programme – a refined version of Modernism. Murcutt however rejects this interpretation. For him the Maison de Verre is a prime instance of what he calls a 'contraption' – a notion broadly similar to Corbusier's machine à habiter, and just as deceptive. 'Contraption' carries for Murcutt no overtones of sophisticated high-techery. On the contrary; a contraption for Murcutt is an instrument finely matched to its changing and complex environment. As host, for instance, Murcutt tunes his house at Kempsey – adjusting its many-louvred skin, and the internal air movements, just so – as if it were a violin. 'I love things that work', he says, **32–36**.

On the whole it is the edges of the Murcutt building – what he calls the ecotone – that 'work' in this way. Inside, the plans – typically attenuated, single-loaded, and imbued with Aalto-meets-Ellwood élan – reappear, slightly modified, time after time.[47] Simple, Calvinist, elegant they work, yes. Often very well indeed. But it is the edges – the screens, the louvres, the sliding and pivoting walls – about which Murcutt becomes impassioned. The skin. The edge is the 'zone of change and excitement', and it is here that the time and money is lavished. The edge is highly worked and multi-layered. Taking the clothing analogy Murcutt speaks almost enviously of Scandinavia, where dramatic seasonal changes allow, in theory at least, 'whole walls to be slid away' in summer. Is there a contradiction between this loving elaboration of the edge, reinforcing difference – and the feathering impulse of eaves and verandah? Not at all, says Murcutt, falling back easily on old-fashioned structural morality; 'the feathered edge is the correct expression for the cantilever', making it clear that any perceived contradiction belies a merely aesthetic interpretation.

The long-standing obsession with 'things that work' is common to many successful architects – not only those who become known as high-tech. What is unusual about Murcutt's obsession is the way in which, again through his upbringing, it has become unified with his equally obsessive and minute responsiveness to conditions on planet Earth.

Murcutt's early academic career was hardly distinguished. 'As a boy', he says, 'I was so dull they sent me at 12 to a school for backward children.' He was, and remains, easily bored,[48] and had to repeat matriculation 'in the days when anybody got into university'. But what did interest him was 'the working of things, the dynamics of things, and above all the geometries of things'. At university, interested at last, he was in the ten per cent of the class that went straight through, although he did fail, of all things, a subject called 'Sunshine and Shade'. This was taught by Ralph Phillips, who wrote the standard Australasian text on the subject, and Murcutt says he was the only student Phillips ever failed. But he also gives that failure huge credit. 'He failed me; he made me understand the geometry of the planet and the sun. And I really do understand it. The buildings come entirely out of Ralph Phillips.'

Other than these few – Chareau, Mies ('I have spent a lifetime trying to get Mies out of my system'), maybe a touch of Frank Lloyd Wright and Ralph Phillips[49] – Murcutt is reluctant to acknowledge lasting influence – from Corb, from Kahn, even from Mies, **37–39**; certainly from any post-Modern architect. He reads little, saying 'I would rather think', and he can think, excluding all other activity, for many hours at a time. Not a natural drawer, he designs in his head, without even putting pencil to paper. This emphasis on individuation and originality is quite unfeigned, and while his egalitarian beliefs oblige him to use the term 'discovery' he is, like his father, pre-eminently an inventor. Architecture, for Murcutt, is an intriguing multi-dimensional problem; the contraption is the solution.

But Murcutt's is not unadulterated Modernism. His frequent use of symmetry as an organizing principle (the Ball-Eastaway house, 1980–83, **40**, the Ken Done house, 1991, **41, 42**), the classical stance and siting

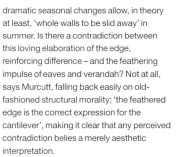

43 Magney house, view from the north of the steel-and-glass elegance of the rear courtyard, with Barragán pool. Landscape design by Sue Barnsley and Andrew McNally.

44–46 Magney house, Paddington.
47 The tiny cottage face of the Magney house, Paddington, gives no clue of the transformation that lies behind.

43

44

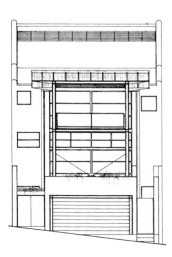

45

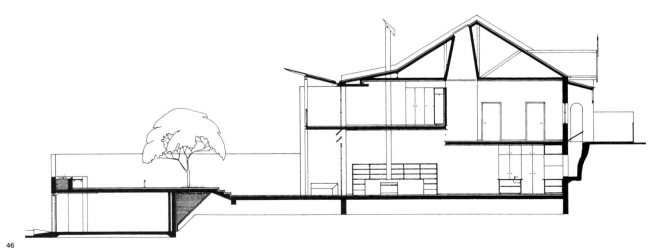

46

47　　　　　　　　　　48

48 The Magney house
had to be fought for
through resistance from
the local council and
from residents; now it
nestles easily into the
terrace-scape.
49 The guest-house,
Kempsey – a tractor
shed becomes the
excuse for 'harmonizing
by confronting' – the
succulent juxtaposition
of old and new.

of the houses, and outright rejection of spatial dynamics ('my interest', says Murcutt, 'is in serenity, like Barragán') would raise any truly Modern eyebrow. Those he most admires, apart from Chareau, are Barragán, Snozzi, Fehn, Scarpa, Aalto, Terragni, Leplastrier: all Modernists with post-Modern appeal, all past-masters of the Hellenic art of contrast; nature and culture, rough and smooth, primitive and refined, old and new; both-and.

Murcutt himself is becoming increasingly skilled in this art of contrast, as the second Magney house in Paddington, **43–48**, and the Kempsey guest-house, **49**, demonstrate. Like those he admires, Murcutt is a Modernist – devout, disciplined, moralistic – whose work has been enriched by, and whose worldwide appeal has in large part depended on post-Modern modes of perception.

In the end, regardless of category or commentary, there can be no doubt that Murcutt has achieved something altogether remarkable. It's not just a question of being local and international, modern and classical, sophisticated and naive. Nor is it just a question of architectonic finesse and ingenuity, although they too are absolutely characteristic of the work. Murcutt has achieved something far less obvious, and far more significant. What he has done, in so hedonistic a culture and so materialistic an age, is to grab centre stage for the invisible issues. His forms, those seductive, irresistible images – however unconsciously derived – have taken top design billing for the lack-lustre questions of environmental control. Yes there are foibles, inconsistencies, delusions; all necessary to the enterprise. And yes, there is an appealing irony in the fact that Murcutt's burgeoning reputation as a 'green' architect rests so heavily not only on the visual appeal of the buildings, but crucially on their refusal to participate, visually, in the landscape.

But to have discovered, and above all to have *sold* the poetry inherent in ventilation, sun control and soil conditions, is a feat even Corb would have envied; even Frank Lloyd Wright. Further, while Murcutt himself may not yearn for the big building, his capacity, through Modernist principle but without Modern dogma, to produce the kinds of dignified and dignifying spaces many Moderns would have given their eye teeth for, has created an international audience eager to see what the results of such a commission might be.

49

50   51

Marie Short house, Kempsey

Set in rolling countryside this house would seem to play the elegant farmhouse to perfection, were it not for the unsettled air, quite contrary to farmhouse expectations of permanence, imparted by its elevation above ground level. The Marie Short house[50] looks like a house that has found its place, but not yet taken it. Murcutt, characteristically, takes a different view. For him this is a house about water, about wind and about an old, weathered landscape, but mostly about water. 'A house in gumboots' is how he describes it, although stilts, or duckboards might be a better metaphor, **50**.

The house sits on near-flat ground above a marshy sub-tropical flood plain; the soil is dense and clayey, natural air movement limited, humidity and rainfall high. It is a soggy environment. The client's requirement of a house as warm in winter and as cool in summer, as standing under the mulberry tree that grew near the original house, necessitated maximum ventilation in summer, sun penetration in winter, **51**, **52**.

To build at grade would have meant an accumulation of groundwater that could keep the area saturated for weeks at a time. 'There is nothing like a dry platform to be working on, in that sort of environment', says Murcutt. 'It is very beautiful.'

Almost as important, for Murcutt, are the snakes. When the floods come, three times a year, the snakes, as well as goannas and other reptiles, head for high ground. In the old house, at grade nearer the river, all doors had to be closed throughout the wet summer season 'because the bloody snakes come in'. Murcutt's admiration for snakes is genuine – he weeps, he says, when the lawnmower slices one concealed in the grass – but it's quite another thing to invite the serpent in. By lifting the house 800–900mm above the ground he has produced a house which the snakes never enter – but beneath which they may lie, preying on the evening congregations of insect-chasing frogs to their hearts' content.

In this way the platform indirectly facilitates what Murcutt has come to recognize as an absolute necessity of life in a wet environment – namely '99 per cent ventilation; on a day of 30°C, with 89 per cent humidity, it's unbearable without'. The platform also actively increases air-flow, he explains, by maximizing the aerofoil effects above and below the house as 'wing' – so that a 2km/hour ambient wind velocity, for instance, gives 3.5km/hour inside the house. Even the orientation of the houses uses the 'geometry of the winds', so that winter westerlies, by contrast, hit the house end-on, and do not produce the same 'aerofoil' effect.

And spatially, is he happy about being so separate from the ground? 'Oh, very much so', he says, citing a Japanese tradition that half a metre (in this case 820mm) above ground is the ideal point from which to observe nature – a sentiment with which awareness of the snake question alone would incline one to concur.

The house has been built in two stages. Stage 1 (1975) consisted of two essentially identical pavilions, each comprising six 3m bays, one bay out-of-synch and divided by a narrow hall.[51] The timber-lined interior has a smooth Scandinavian feel,[52] contrasting pleasurably with the weathered exterior. The plan is simple; very workable, very open. Only bedrooms and bathrooms are enclosed. The 1980 extension added a bedroom, storage and the southern sitting room (with a fireplace since this is the cold side of the house) and strengthened the connection between it and the living/dining area, at the western end of which the outdoor room, veiled against insects, remains unaltered.

The integration of kitchen and living has become something of an article of faith for Murcutt, ever since he used the device in renovating his own house in 1969[53] which was even then, he says, regarded in Australia as something 'really avant garde'. The change in attitudes Murcutt puts down to post-war Mediterranean immigration, and to feminism, but whatever the reason, the change is here to stay as far as Murcutt is concerned. In this regard the Kempsey house demonstrates 'as good a relationship in food preparation, in entertainment and being with people as I have ever done. I don't think I will ever better it in my lifetime. It is so – for me – perfect a relationship'.

Thoreau, one can only surmise, would have wholeheartedly approved. 'These days a man does not admit you to his hearth, but has got the mason to build one for yourself somewhere in his alley, and hospitality is the art of keeping you at the greatest distance. There is as much secrecy about the cooking as if he had a design to poison you … It would seem as if the very language of our parlours would degenerate into parlaver wholly … its metaphors and tropes are necessarily so far-fetched… .'[54]

The spatial ordering of the house – the play between symmetry and asymmetry,[55] and between casualness and discipline – gives the living spaces a versatility which is remarkable, especially within Modernism, but quite characteristic of Murcutt's work. Be they bare-footed or dinner-suited, the room accommodates and dignifies its inhabitants with equal ease. Murcutt's interest in what he calls 'serenity', his rejection of tension and spatial movement as interest-creating devices, are instrumental here. '*People* are the objects in the spaces', he says.

'My buildings are about making people look good, and feel good.' And that is precisely what they do.

54   **55**

Magney house, Bingie Point, Moruya

53 Magney house,
Bingie Point: an
uncompromising house
in an uncompromising
landscape.
54 Detail of a gutter.
55 External adjustable
metal blinds protect the
north-facing glass wall.

The house at Moruya is unusual in the Murcutt iconography in having a roof which is predominantly concave, not convex, **53**. This is the product of various factors, all of them related in some way to the site, which is remote, exposed, starkly beautiful. Such factors include a stated desire on the part of the clients, who had for many years camped on the site, to preserve the light-roofed sense of being under canvas (a normal pitched roof might have looked like a tent, but would not have had the same psychological impact, says Murcutt); a need to collect water, **54**, and a desire to do it as economically as possible (one gutter instead of two); a sculptural response to the landscape's folded forms (the eaves on both sides parallel the slope of the ground at that point); and a need, especially here where the wind-exposure made wholesale ventilation less than desirable, to exclude summer sun, but admit it in winter.

In response to this last requirement, and to dramatic views over lake and coast, the house is oriented due north.[60] This allowed the roof to be clipped just at the equinox cut-off sun angle, so that no sun enters the house in summer at all, despite the unprotected clerestory glazing on that north wall (the lower glazing being protected by external adjustable metal blinds, **55**). In winter, by contrast, there is sun all day – climbing half way up the back

wall – says the proud client – at breakfast time, in mid-winter.

Unlike Kempsey, where the problem is to keep cool and keep dry, the dominant concerns at Moruya were to provide protection from the wind and from cool winter nights. The house at Moruya, therefore, where the slope and soil conditions obviate water table problems, sits on an insulated slab at grade. The slab and the back, brick wall of the house act as a thermal sink, warmed by the winter sun (or artificially when need be).

Further, although both houses are modular, the size of the module varies according to the perceived scale of the landscape. Moruya's wild open spaces demanded a module of 4.7m, compared with 3.0m at cultivated Kempsey – and this in turn, says Murcutt, specified a change in structural material from timber to steel. The cladding too was chosen at least in part as a visual response to the site, its zinc-coated and anodized silvers picking up the colours of the grass which Murcutt describes as 'tufted, tough silver with a touch of brown'.

The plan too, all similarities to the Murcutt norm notwithstanding, responds to sun and site – at least insofar as the living rooms are strung out enfilade along sun and view. Here, as ever, Murcutt simply applies the standard set of principles to a

particular problem. The linear division of the plan, again, this time into servant, circulation and living zones succinctly promotes legibility, spatial order and environmental control. The clients had expected something deeper, but are unequivocal in their conviction that the linear arrangement is superior (they worried even then, they say, about how to get sun into south-facing bedrooms).

As at the Ball-Eastaway house, the entrance is consciously understated[61] – apparently at the client's request. Like that house, too, the Magney house is comparatively small, and the legibility principle is rigorously applied. This is immensely satisfying, both aesthetically and intellectually. But even once you're in, one cannot but wonder how to get *in* to a house like this. This is a question not of entry, but of withdrawing. A question, to use Murcutt terminology, of prospect and refuge. What price refuge, in this elegant but inhospitable landscape? Not only does the house make no attempt to snuggle in ('my architecture *is* confronting'), but nor is there any real withdrawing space in the house, nothing emphatically *in*, other than a tiny underground wine cellar, which is approached down a short ladder from inside a cupboard.

The plan is characteristically linear, both in form and in its primary divisions, with

servant spaces lined up along the back (south) wall, and served along the front, with circulation space, as delineated by the only slightly oppressive valley (gutter), running between. It is very clear, the entire house intelligible at a glance. Is it perhaps too clear? Have the minimalism, the discipline, the legibility principle – the Modernism, in fact – resulted in a loss of mystery, a loss of complexity to mirror human nature? Has Murcutt inherited the foible of which Venturi, quoting Rudolph, accused Mies van der Rohe, namely, problem-solving by oversimplification?[62] Are particular clients being moulded to fit Murcutt's generalized, Quakerish reinterpretation of the Thoreau ideal, a house where 'nothing was hidden; it was an honest expression of a human's life, in very simple terms'?

Murcutt argues that people tend to have fairly standard and basically fairly simple requirements of their houses. 'People want to prepare food. People want to eat food. People want to sit down and talk with one another…' This may itself sound over-generalized, but the fact remains that the clients were, and remain, delighted with the house; so pleased in fact and so dissatisfied, by comparison, with their town house, that they commissioned Murcutt to design them another new house, in Paddington. Who could cavil at that?

56, 57 Ball-Eastaway house: the galvanized corrugated steel gives a grey finish, which Murcutt prefers to the silver of zinc-allume. **58** The house appears as a spaceship landed in the bush.

The Ball-Eastaway house stands even higher off the ground. Whereas the elevation of the Marie Short house was impelled by wet conditions, the Ball-Eastaway house, built in sparse sclerophyll woodland on the ancient sandstone plateau to Sydney's north, is informed by dryness.

But the principles are similar. To build on the rock would raise the water table, rotting the roots of the yellow bloodwoods above the house, and creating a water shadow which would destroy the bush for up to 40m in its lee. Murcutt was determined to 'allow the water to move over the rock shelf in exactly the same way as it has for thousands of years'. Perched like a foreign vessel in one of this fragile continent's most fragile ecosystems, the house alters nothing, says Murcutt, but the shadow pattern.[56]

Everything else runs from this primary response to the site. Specifically positioning the house on the least sensitive part of the site, Murcutt allowed the patterns of the dissected sandstone to suggest a narrow plan whose linearity is emphasized by a careful alignment of the walls to allow long views, and only long views, through the house. The oblique entrance-bridge was a way – indeed, he suggests, the only way – of entering without walking either on the rock face or up and over it 'like you do in the London Underground', says Murcutt, 'which I hated'.

Directly opposite the entrance is the meditation deck; this back-to-back 'puncturing' of the private realm being aligned with the directional flow, so to speak, of the rock shelf beneath, which 'dives into the building on one side', as Murcutt describes it, and 'pushes out' at the point where, on the other side of the main 'gallery' wall, the meditation deck 'thrusts into the trees'.

This meditation deck occurs at what is for Murcutt the most private part of the site, its distant views giving a sense of abstraction diminished elsewhere by the intimate proximity and busyness of nature. The deck itself is in fact rather less than thrusting, being wholly within the body of the house but, with five faces wholly opaque and the remaining one lacking so much as a rail to separate the human from the sparse, dry distance, it is undeniably private – almost (for the non-meditant) to the point of claustrophobia.

Murcutt is in fact passionately opposed to decks which thrust beyond the building – 'they're not about living', he says – and is apt to launch into a well-rehearsed spiel on the importance of prospect and refuge at the mere suggestion. Arguably in fact the flat-roofed side-aisles (which Murcutt calls the 'ears' of the house) with their assiduously defined edges, are precisely about being in the landscape, without being in it; the vault by itself would have been too contained, says Murcutt. The ears 'gave it a freedom', he says, and a place for the paintings between the human world and the landscape. They also, intentionally or otherwise, carry classical compositional overtones which reinforce the building's temple-like stance with regard to nature.

Sydney Ball, the client, is a painter, and the rather unnerving depth of the meditation deck (twice that of the 'ears' which might be expected to accommodate such a space) was determined by the height of and minimum viewing distance for the biggest (2.5 x 6m) of the pre-existing paintings for which the house was required to provide hanging space. Would Murcutt have given the house more lateral transparency if he could? 'No. I liked all that openness of landscape, and suddenly being taken right away from it, into a painting.'

Open at both ends the house thus became an extruded form, emphatically directional. Reluctance to cut any trees meant it had to be eased in between existing flora, but the suggestion of infinite linear extension is there, and provides the compositional leitmotif for the entire house.[57] Heightened

56   57

by such devices as the precise alignment of the southern dividing wall on an existing tree (allowing both bedrooms to share its amenity), this longitudinal emphasis informs everything, from the axial symmetry of both plan and form, to the peeled fingers of barge and verandah-end details.

Here at last, the Romantic might feel, is something romantic, something of the Arts and Crafts. But it would be a mistake to understand these unravellings as any attempt to meld visually with the landscape, rather they consciously stress the linearity of the *parti* – an idea drawn from the landscape, yes, but in itself still abstract, preconceived and in this sense an applied Rationalist discipline.

Within this fundamental formal discipline, the rest of the thinking is characteristically rational. The house is in a fire zone, so timber is used sparingly (floor joists only) and finished with retardant paint, while walls and roof are structured and clad in steel, **56, 57**. Murcutt explains that this is the most vulnerable part of any building, since 'what mostly happens' in a bush fire is that a burning gum leaf catches in a gutter and burns up into the roof; the curved roof form was cheap and spatially pleasant, but crucially gives no lodging place for leaves, while the gutters, too, seemingly oversized for a parched climate, are in fact a direct response. During a fire these broad, tapering dishes, which Murcutt likens to a dry creek bed, are filled by the sprinkler system[58]: in normal times their tapering sides and the funnel-headed down-pipes are designed to use the centrifugal flow of water to solve the notorious tendency of eucalypt leaves to clog any available opening by turning the leaves on-end… truncated to make a heap at the bottom… an idea 'both romantic, poetic at one level, and hellishly rational at another level'. 'I actually think it's a very reasonable building', says Murcutt. 'As a tough building in a tough landscape, I think it is appropriate. That's all I'm interested in. Not international standard. I am looking for a standard that is appropriate to its place.'

More than that, in fact, it's a very clever building – finding a way of surviving in an environment which lifts not a finger to help. What it is not, by any stretch of the imagination, is a primitive hut.[59] The relationship between the house and its environment is profound, but operates only at the most abstract, analytical level. One's reservations, such as they are, spring in the main from this abstraction – the absolute formal, visual and spatial separateness of house and environment, only underlined by the tenuous and oblique tethering bridge, the unforgiving asceticism of the meditation deck, the lack of interior complication. But there can be no doubt that as a sensitive environmental object, and as a delightful jewel in its own right, this is an immensely sophisticated piece of work, **58**.

Marie Short house

'A house in gumboots',
says Murcutt – wise
attire under the
circumstances: sleeping
on the floor in these
bedrooms one hears the
serpents feast on frogs.
Right, verandah gable.

Marie Short house

Ceiling and wall details in the kitchen and living space. Screens and filters (not to mention the constant awareness of snakes and other assorted wildlife) ensure that inside is emphatically inside, reinforcing the distinction just as they dissolve it.

Marie Short house

The outdoor room, looking west. Sections of the wall become pivoting doors between the two parallel pavilions: a crossing (beneath the box gutter) between naves. The kitchen/dining relationship has an understated spatial elegance equally accommodating of bare feet or dinner jackets: 'as good a relationship', says Murcutt, 'as I have ever done'.

Marie Short house

The tractor shed-cum-guest-house, Kempsey. Left, the corner shower box opens to intimations of nature (well above snake level). Right, sheer delight in the found Palladian plan and the opportunity to bring the rusticity and refinement into stark contrast.

Magney house

Magney house

Right, a north-facing glass wall, but the summer sun is carefully excluded by eaves which are cut precisely to ensure that the sun is never incident upon the unprotected upper glazing until after the equinox.

Magney house

Gutter detail and the house at sunset. Far right, the spinal circulation space is oppressive in order to emphasize the uplift and openness either side.

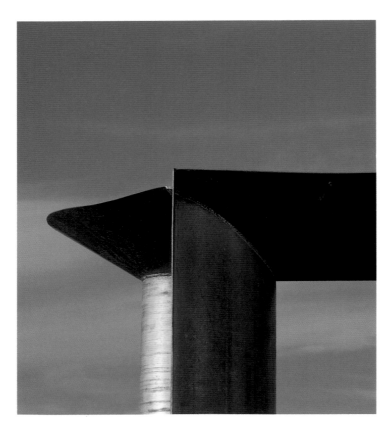

Magney house

Ball-Eastaway house

Right, the house is perched with great delicacy in one of this fragile continent's most fragile ecosystems. Far right, the meditation deck – an eerie absence of diversions, like an anechoic chamber. The ceiling demonstrates what has become a point of faith with Murcutt, namely the use of mini-corrugated steel in 'interior' spaces such as this, where humans are in close contact.

Oversized gutters
allow gum leaves
to swirl down end-on,
preventing the kind
of blockage which, with
these oily, inflammable
leaves, can be a matter
of life-and-death in
cases of bushfire;
in such a fire specially-
designed plugs let the
gutters fill with water.
Murcutt delights in this
sort of technological
poetry, likening the
system to 'a dry
creek bed'.
Above, an exterior
light switch on the
meditation deck.

Ball-Eastaway house

Unlike the meditation deck, the north-facing deck is friendly, relaxed and comparatively intimate in its relationship with the bush: does the deliberate paring of the edges contradict the house's otherwise emphatic separateness from its landscape? Not at all, says Murcutt. The peeled fingers are about linearity, like the rock formations beneath – not about merging in.

The linear nature
of the house is further
underscored by the tree
on which it is axially
aligned, dead centre,
so that it is 'shared'
equally by the bedrooms.
Far right, the living
room looking north
into the bush.

Marie Short house

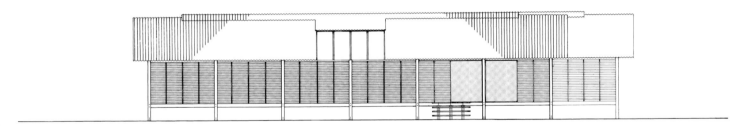

North elevation

Ground floor plan

(original version)

1 screened verandah
2 living room
3 dining room
4 kitchen
5 farm utility area
6 bedroom
7 verandah
8 wc
9 shower
10 dressing room
11 pergola

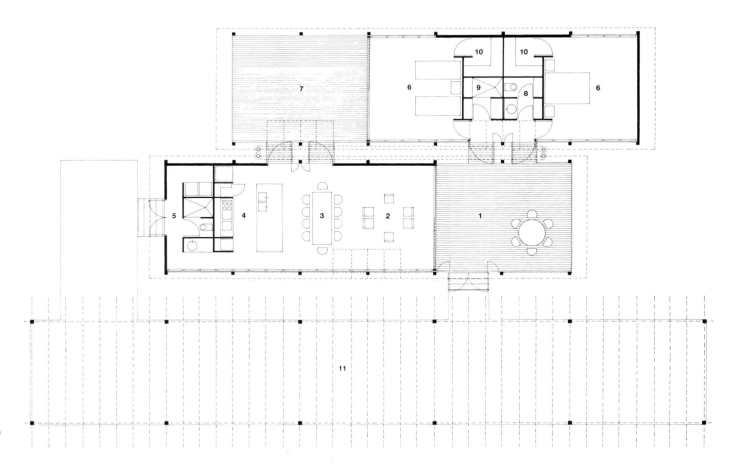

| 0 | 3 metres |
| 0 | 9 feet |

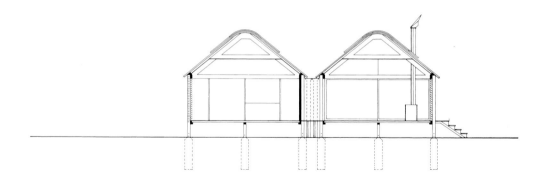

Ground floor plan

(1981/82 version)

1 screened verandah
2 living room
3 dining room
4 kitchen
5 bedroom
6 sitting room
7 verandah
8 wc
9 shower
10 store
11 dressing room
12 laundry room

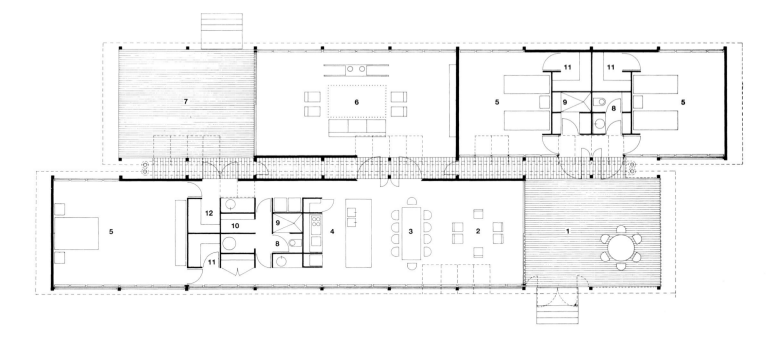

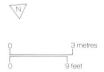

0   3 metres

0   9 feet

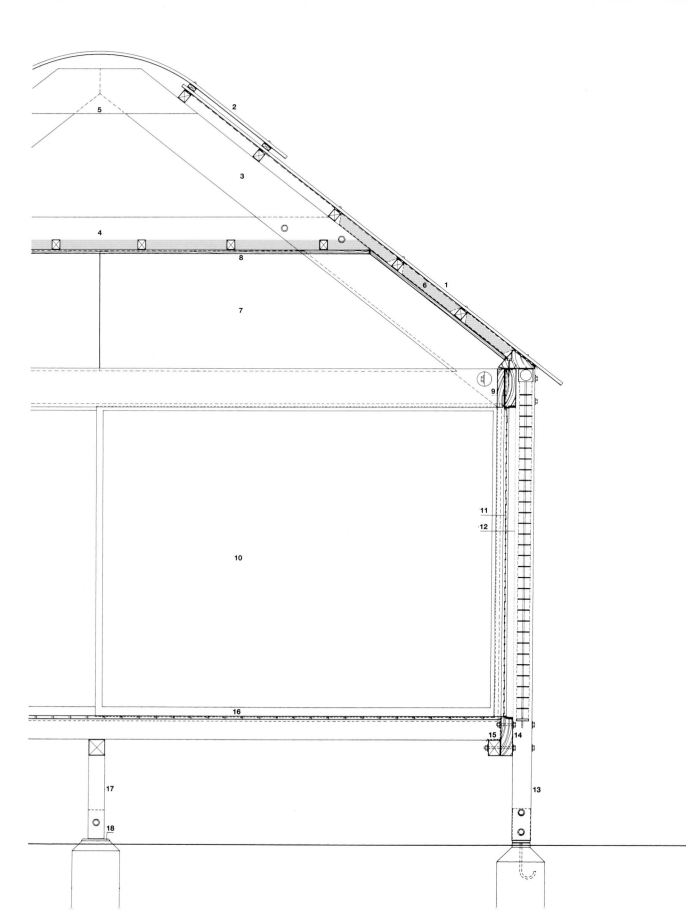

Detail section

1 corrugated galvanized steel roofing with UNISIL filler strip
2 upper roof, raised on 32mm timber battens allowing flutes to act as vents, bird proofed
3 250 x 75mm Oregon white oak rafter
4 Oregon white oak collar tie bolted to rafters
5 plywood gusset
6 75mm insulation on double-sided sisalation
7 6mm drawn glass, silicon rubber jointed, bedded in non-set pigmented mastic
8 timber-boarded ceiling, insulated
9 38mm fascia board
10 glazed sliding door
11 100mm wide baked enamel steel louvres
12 insect mesh stretched between aluminium flats rebated into frame
13 125 x 125mm timber post bolted to steel base plate on 300mm diameter x 1.8 metre deep concrete foundation
14 hardwood fascia beam bolted to posts
15 flashing on open decks
16 stained timber boarded floor on 125 x 50mm hardwood joists
17 100 x 100mm hardwood bearer on posts
18 ant cap

0   300mm

0   12 inches

Firebox detail

1 modified standard
  jetmaster firebox
2 steel casing on
  20 x 20mm framing,
  painted black
  enamel
3 gravel heat bank
4 stainless steel inner
  flue, single length
5 250mm diameter
  steel outer flue,
  single length, painted
  black enamel
6 vent holes
7 woodstore

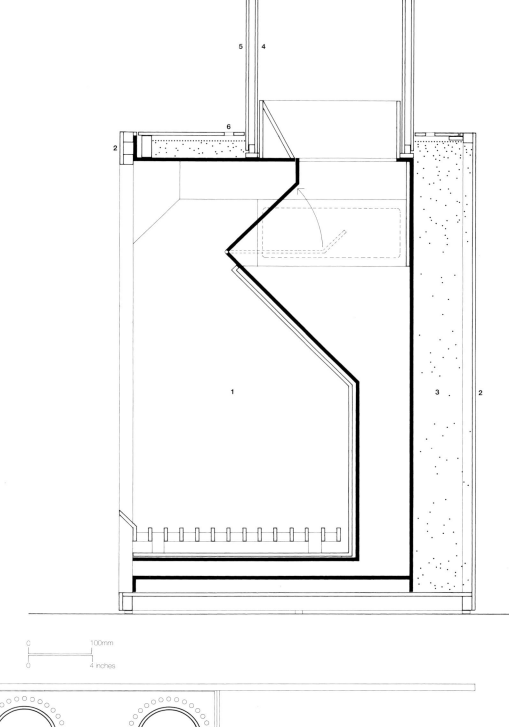

| 0 | 250mm |
| 0 | 9 inches |

| 0 | 100mm |
| 0 | 4 inches |

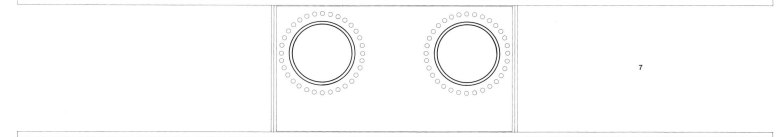

Magney house

Ground floor plan

1 bedroom
2 wc/shower
3 kitchen
4 sitting/dining room
5 court
6 family room
7 wc
8 shower
9 laundry
10 general purpose
   room/garage
11 rainwater downpipe

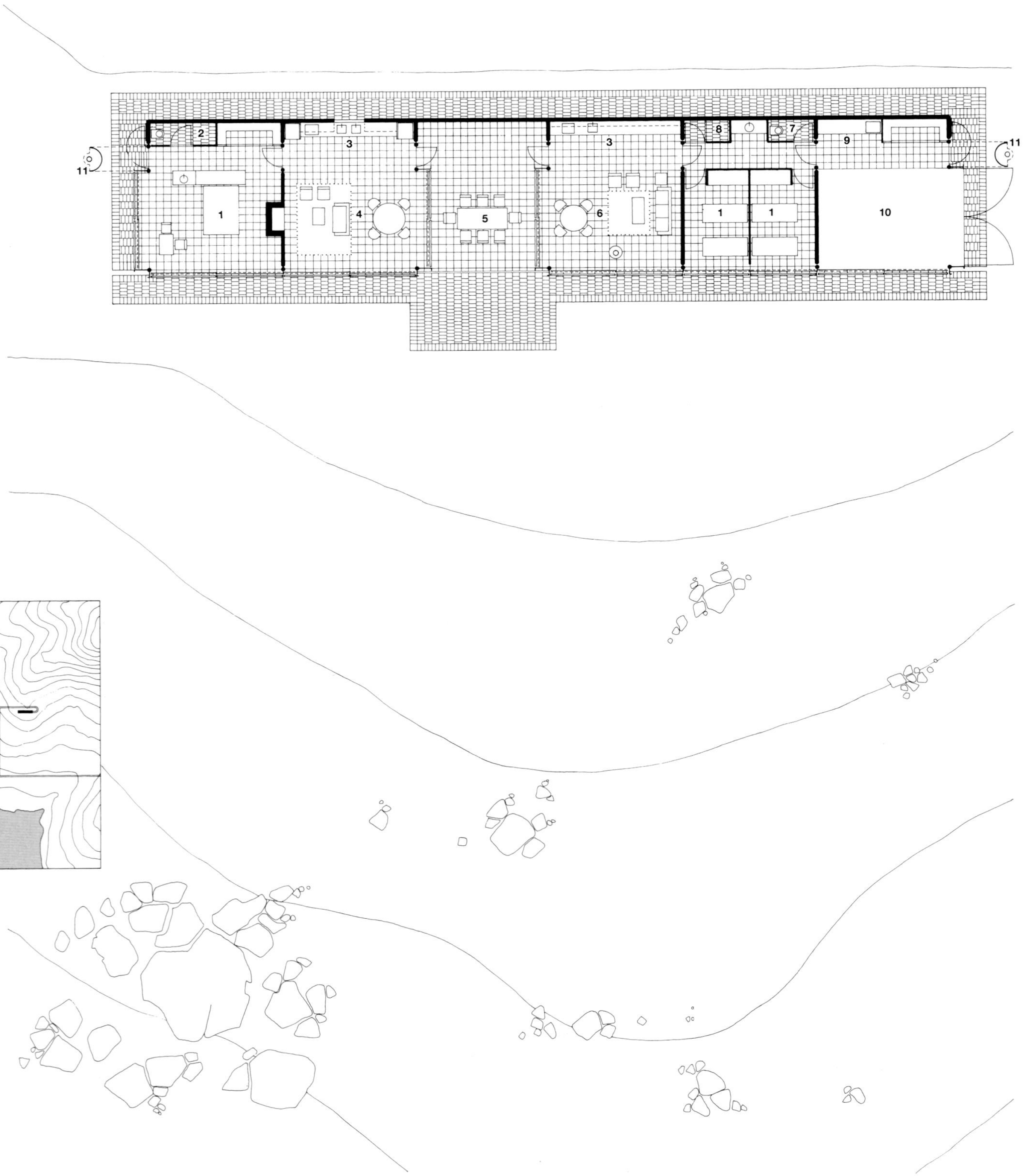

N

| 0 | | | 5 metres |
| 0 | | | 15 feet |

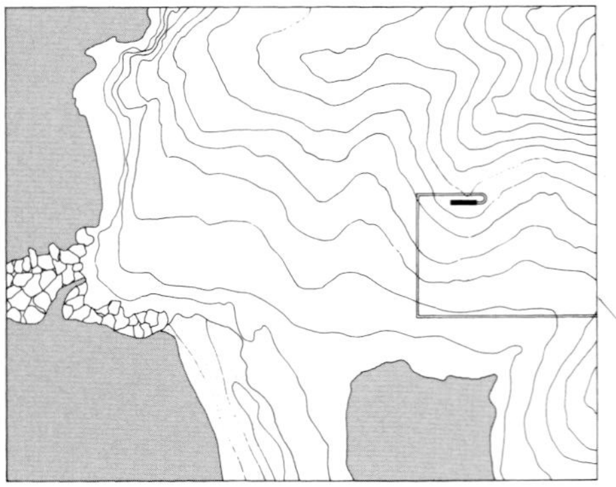

Location

| 0 | | 300 metres |
| 0 | | 300 yards |

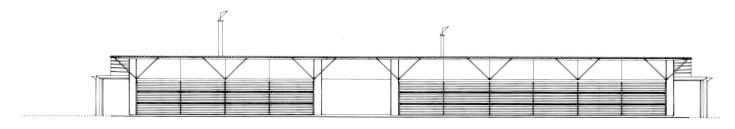

North elevation

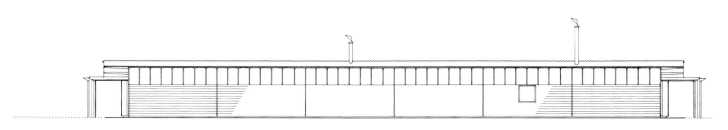

South elevation

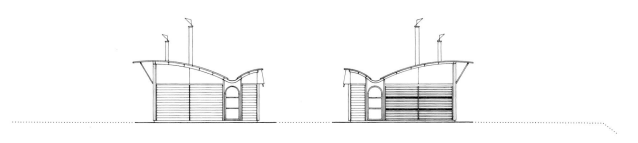

West elevation

East elevation

0   5 metres

0   15 feet

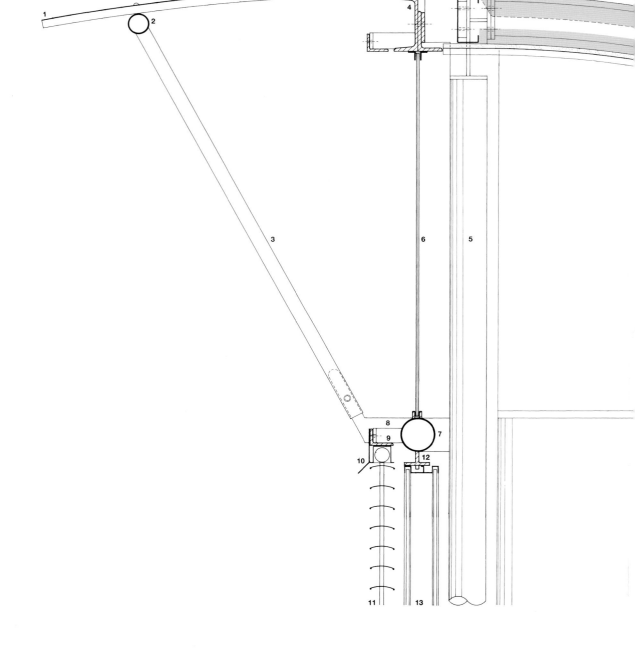

Detail section

1 corrugated galvanized steel roofing with UNISIL filler strip
2 60mm diameter galvanized steel tube continuous support
3 42mm diameter galvanized steel strut welded to tube and bolted to bottom bracket
4 continuous perimeter channel and angle welded to 10mm steel plate fabricated bracket
5 114mm diameter hollow section steel column
6 fixed glazing, silicon jointed
7 114mm diameter hollow section transom
8 10mm plate transom/strut bracket welded to column
9 blind box angle support and bracket
10 aluminium cover to blind box
11 venetian blinds operated from inside
12 cut steel T welded to transom
13 glazed sliding doors

14 114mm diameter hollow section steel curved roof beam
15 75mm insulation hung on double-sided sisalation on chicken wire
16 50mm ceiling insulation
17 zinc coated C-section purlins
18 10mm plasterboard ceiling with control joints
19 aluminium gutter
20 114mm diameter hollow section steel beam
21 aluminium glazing system
22 timber vent on friction hinge sitting in aluminium angle frame on brackets fixed back to brickwork, insect meshed, operated by hooked rod
23 reinforced brickwork wall with 3mm hard plaster finish on 10mm render internally
24 corrugated galvanized steel wall lining end-sealed using UNISIL filler strip, insulated

0   200mm

0   8 inches

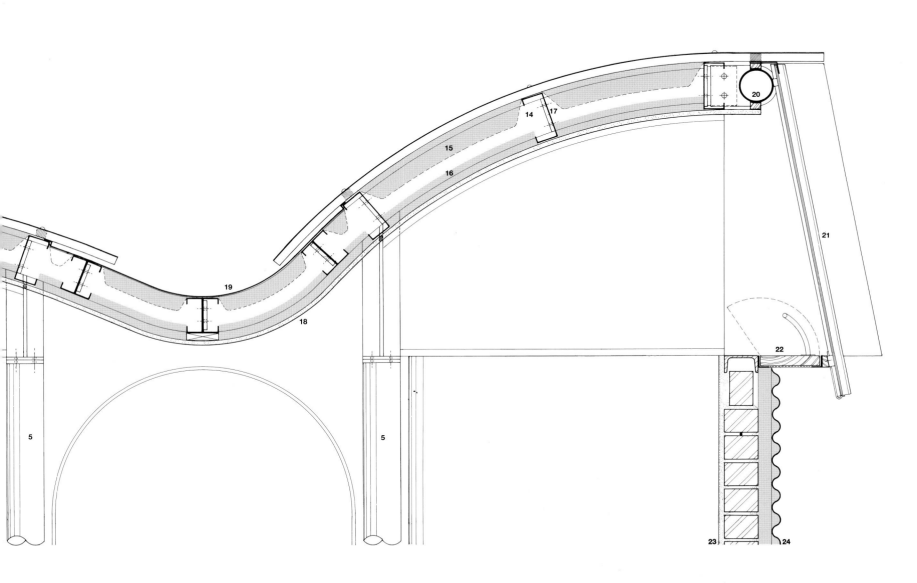

Ball-Eastaway house

Ground floor plan

1 bedroom
2 study
3 verandah
4 bathroom
5 laundry room
6 hall
7 dining room
8 kitchen
9 living room
10 pantry

| 0 | | 5 metres |
| 0 | | 15 feet |

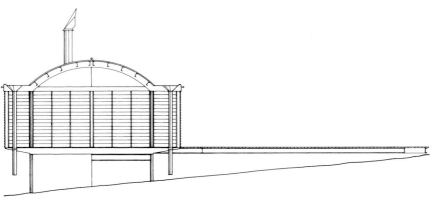

South-west elevation

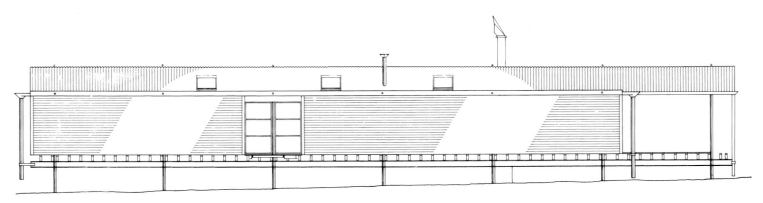

South-east elevation

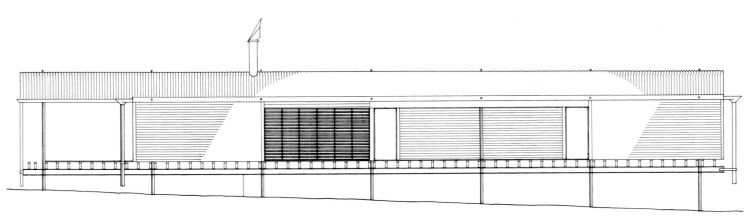

0   3 metres   **North-west elevation**

0   9 feet

Detail section

1. corrugated galvanized steel roofing with UNISIL filler strip
2. zinc-coated C section purlins between curved mild steel roof beams
3. drenching outlet
4. 12mm plasterboard ceiling
5. double-glazed rooflight
6. heavy duty roofing felt membrane on plywood gutter
7. galvanized wire gutter guard
8. 75mm insulation and double-sided sisalation supported on chicken wire
9. steel beam welded to top of column
10. 102mm diameter hollow section column
11. galvanized steel capping
12. 6mm clear glass
13. 75mm galvanized steel stud wall, insulated
14. corrugated galvanized steel wall lining end-sealed using UNISIL filler strip, pressed metal corners
15. torgued and grooved floor boards
16. 250 x 75mm hardwood floor joists
17. 250mm universal beam between columns
18. mini corrugated iron soffit
19. glazed ceramic tiles

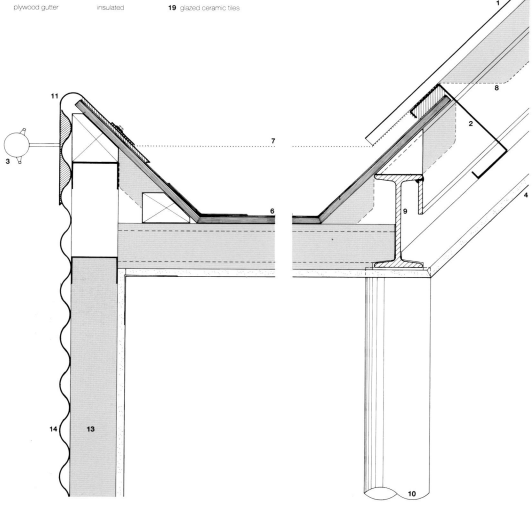

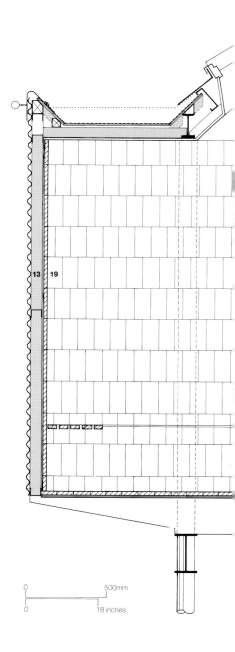

0 ⊢⊣ 100mm

0 ⊢⊣ 4 inches

0 ⊢⊣ 500mm

0 ⊢⊣ 18 inches

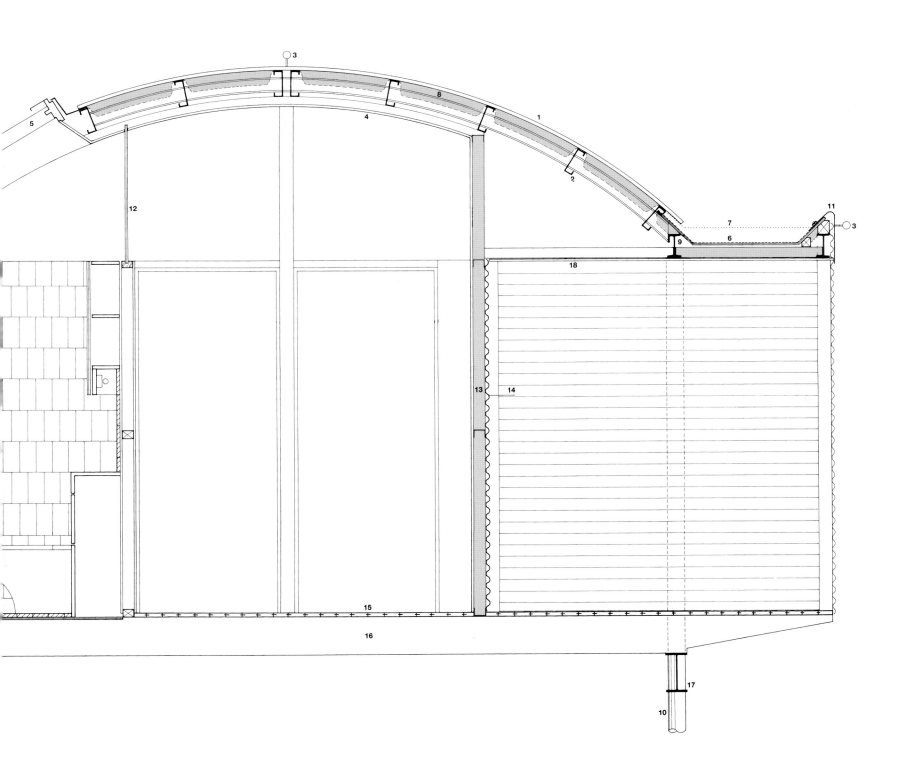

Bibliography

Beck, Haig and **Cooper, Jackie** 'Glenn Murcutt; Silver City Museum Broken Hill', *UME*, Box 1 Portfolio 1, University of Melbourne, 1992.

Drew, Philip *Leaves of Iron: Glenn Murcutt; Pioneer of an Australian Architectural Form*, The Law Book Company, Sydney, 1985.

Griggs, Michael and **McGregor, Craig** (eds) *Australian Built: Responding to the Place*, Australia Council, 1985.

Krutch, J.W. (ed.) *Thoreau; Walden and other Writings*, Bantam Books, New York, 1962.

Credits

Marie Short house
Kempsey NSW, 1974–75
Engineer: E.R. (Dick) Taylor, Taylor Thomson Whitting

Ball-Eastaway house
Glenorie NSW, 1980–83
Assistant: Graham Jahn
Engineer: Taylor Payne McDonald

Magney house
Bingie Point, Moruya NSW, 1983–84
Engineer: James Taylor, James Taylor and Associates

Notes

1 The 1992 Australian *Who's Who* continues to restrict its architectural menage to the Seidlers, Harry and Penelope, who have an entry each: Murcutt regularly declines invitations to be included for privacy reasons, he says.

2 Craig McGregor, 'A Shed Above the Rest', *The Sydney Morning Herald*, 31 October 1992, p.43.

3 Haig Beck and Jackie Cooper, 'Glenn Murcutt; Silver City Museum Broken Hill', *UME*, Box 1 Portfolio 1, 1992. The essay does not pursue this line, presenting Murcutt instead as a 'rationalist'; nor does it draw the important distinction outlined in note 7, employing 'rationalist' simply to mean one who is 'rational'.

4 Profile of Murcutt by Dennis Sharp in *Building Design*, No. 933, April 21 1989, pp.28–9.

5 Murcutt's lecture to the RIBA, reported by John Pardey in *Building Design*, No. 934, April 28 1989, p.2.

6 Article on the Ken Done house, in the wealthy Sydney suburb of Mosman (hardly outback); *Building Design*, No. 1104, November 27 1992, pp.16–17.

7 There is an important distinction to be drawn between Rationalism, in its technical philosophical sense, and rationalism as an everyday term. Where the latter simply denotes a commitment to reason and experience over belief (and is more akin to positivism, or even empiricism), Rationalism, which might be more properly termed *a priorism*, signifies a view that truth is accessible through reason alone, independent of worldly experience. Rationality – or reason – is regarded on the one hand as a tool to knowledge, on the other as its only proper source. This latter view clearly embraces the possibility of belief, but excludes empiricism – and thus is in fundamental disagreement with empirically-based belief systems usually considered to be rational, such as Western science. It clearly tends also to universalism.

8 Presented to Murcutt in Helsinki on 24 October 1992; members of the medal committee were Professor Kenneth Frampton (US), Professor Sverre Fehn (Norway), Professor Juhani Pallasmaa, (Finland); architects Pentti Kareoja (Finland) and Ms Gunnel Adlercreutz (President, Finnish Association of Architects); and Aimo Murtomaki (Finnish Ministry of Education).

9 All quotations, unless otherwise stated, are taken from three discussions between the author and Glenn Murcutt on 11, 18 and 23 November 1992.

10 Murcutt's foreword to Philip Drew, *Leaves of Iron: Glenn Murcutt: Pioneer of an Australian Architectural Form*, The Law Book Company, Sydney, 1985, p.7.

11 The obvious corollary, as an area for speculation, is to ask 'where is Murcutt going?', but Murcutt himself flatly denies any progression within his oeuvre (from Mies to Barragán, for instance, or from Modern to post-Modern, lightweight to solid, whatever), any influence from world intellectual currents, and any ambition towards a particular type of work – reiterating his responsiveness to the site, above all, and his determination, learned like so much else from his father, to 'do ordinary things extraordinarily well'.

12 For instance, by Philip Drew, op. cit. Drew refers constantly to Thoreau but nowhere says clearly why.

13 Krutch, p.111. This is probably Thoreau's most famous single remark.

14 Krutch, op. cit., p.131.

15 Thoreau's actual words were, 'Simplicity, simplicity, simplicity! I say let your affairs be as two or three, and not a hundred or a thousand... Simplify, simplify. Instead of three meals a day, if it be necessary eat but one...'. Krutch, op. cit., p.173. He bemoans the way in which 'our life is frittered away by detail'.

16 Now the capital of Papua New Guinea (350 km from Lae).

17 In speaking of his ability, for instance, to 'read' a site in terms of its water table, drainage characteristics, soil qualities etc. Murcutt says, without pretension, 'at that level I am very much in tune with the land...'.

18 Murcutt insists on the term 'discovery' rather than invention – believing the latter to be elitist and misguided. 'Everything exists', he says. 'The biggest task architects have is to discover it. I don't believe in invention. Invention privatizes it. I think anybody can do what I'm doing, with effort. It's just a matter of patience.'

19 This may be Sam Murcutt's expression, but it has a very Thoreau flavour to it.

20 Krutch, op. cit., p.285.

21 Designed and built in Paris 1928–32 by Pierre Chareau and his little-acknowledged Dutch collaborator, architect Bernard Bijvoet.

22 Such as the Littlemore house, Paddington, or the Ken Done house, Mosman.

23 The Magney house, Paddington, that won a Royal Australian Institute of Architects (NSW Chapter) merit award in 1991 (and Commendation in the National Awards 1992), was entered at the specific invitation of the jury.

24 In fact this isn't quite true. Murcutt has employed associates on particular projects – such as Wendy Lewin on the Littlemore house, Paddington (1983–85), Graham Jahn on the Ball-Eastaway house and Reg Lark on the Ken Done house, Mosman, 1991. Furthermore some domestic projects – such as his adaptive re-use of the 19th century Raheen in Melbourne – have been enormous, while other large projects, such as the Silver City Museum, Broken Hill, have been entirely documented by Murcutt and one other (in this case Reg Lark). On the whole, though, he works determinedly alone.

25 The Nicholas and Carruthers houses at Mt Irvine cost A$40,000 and A$45,000 respectively (1980).

26 The analogy is meant presumably to emphasize Seidler's unshakeable strength of purpose, rather than to denote his understanding of the urban fabric – which is of course profoundly opposed to Haussman's.

27 Murcutt in Philip Drew, op. cit., p.7.

28 Murcutt is quoting here Frank Lloyd Wright's 'Credo' from *The Natural House* by Frank Lloyd Wright, Horizon Press, New York, 1954.

29 Thoreau, 'On the Duty of Civil Disobedience', 1849 in Krutch (ed.) op. cit.

30 Murcutt in Philip Drew, op. cit., p.7.

31 See for instance J.V. de Sousa, 'Realist Architecture in the Australian Idiom: The Work of Glenn Murcutt', *Centre*, Volume 4, 1988, p.90–99. 'What strikes one most about these buildings are their simple honesty and integrity – true to the architect, true to the owner, true to themselves and true to the Australian landscape in which they sit.'

32 Murcutt in Philip Drew, op. cit., p.7.

33 Murcutt says the phrase came to him from a Western Australian architect, Brian Klopper, in 1983. In his 1984 foreword to Philip Drew, op. cit., Murcutt writes of his delight 'to learn only last year that there is a saying amongst Aboriginals "one must touch this earth lightly"...', weakening assertions sometimes made that the phrase originated in Bruce Chatwin's *Songlines*, Jonathan Cape Ltd, 1987.

34 Quoted for instance by de Sousa, op.cit., p.91.

35 This metaphor bears no relation, says Murcutt, to Thoreau's observation 'still we live meanly, like ants; though the fable tells us we were long ago changed into men...'. Krutch, op. cit., p.173.

36 The native Australian name for a small, primitive or ramshackle dwelling.

37 The Kempsey site is in fact classified as warm temperate, with sub-tropical pockets.

38 For example on a 'fabulous project' for a desert museum in Arizona.

39 Craig McGregor, op. cit.

40 The Robin Boyd Award was given in 1981 to the two Mt Irvine houses. *Architecture Australia*, awards issue, Vol. 70, no. 6, December 1981, p.10.

41 Michael Griggs and Craig McGregor (eds) *Australian Built: Responding to the Place*, Australia Council, 1985, p.14.

42 Craig McGregor, op. cit.

43 Craig McGregor, op. cit.

44 This was of course the standard anthropological view until quite recently.

45 These days Murcutt uses only pitched roofs, saying 'people can put up with a lot, even imperfect planning, but they cannot tolerate a drop of water into the house'. The voice of experience.

46 Murcutt slips constantly into use of the term 'invention', despite his conscious preference for 'discovery', which starts to look like a choice based on socio-ethical beliefs, rather than architectural or epistemological ones.

47 Beck and Cooper argue convincingly however that the linear plan is not produced to formula, but hard-won from first principles each time, during Murcutt's 'laborious, analytic design process'. Haig Beck and Jackie Cooper, op. cit., p.3.

48 Even now he gives the need for a high turnover of clients as one main reason for maintaining a domestic practice.

49 Even Barragan, much-cited by Murcutt, remains on his list of admirees, rather than influences.

50 Still so called, in spite of the fact that the house, built for Marie Short, is now owned by Murcutt and his wife.

51 This basic *parti* remains unchanged, despite the subsequent additions, which simply lengthened the house.

52 Philip Drew proposes Mies as the general source of Murcutt's standard longitudinal pavilion plan, and the Farnsworth house in particular as the prototype for Marie Short's house, on the basis of the basic composition of two staggered platforms. Philip Drew, op. cit., pp.74 and 84–5. Beyond that however similarities are superficial, at best.

53 The Wunda Road house, Mosman, Sydney.

54 Krutch, op. cit., p.286.

55 Murcutt's use of symmetry is immensely sophisticated: sometimes establishing symmetrical spatial sequences (such as the main living/eating space in the Short house) within an overall asymmetry, and at other times allowing asymmetry to operate within a predominantly symmetrical spatial and structural skeleton, as at the Ball-Eastaway house. The effect is to endow Murcutt with this vast flexibility in terms of register, for which Modernism frequently strove, but which it achieved only rarely, being forced often to rely for a sense of formality on the use of expensive materials. In jettisoning Modern dogma Murcutt has bought himself the liberty to out-Modern the Moderns.

56 In fact, one rock did have to be cut to allow the installation of a septic tank.

57 Such linearity is also very un-Miesian, making nonsense for instance of Philip Drew's rather tentative comparison with the Barcelona Pavilion. Philip Drew, op. cit., p.128.

58 This is an economical version of the Laurie Short house, whose entire concrete roof is ponded, as well as having sprinklers trained on the surrounding bush. The Laurie Short house was well tested when during a bush fire the owner rolled 'our 44 gallon drums of petrol from the shed into the living room and sat with them while the fire passed over them, leaving the house, and occupants, untouched.

59 See Philip Drew's assertion that the Aboriginal bark shelter suggests 'a special connection between bark and corrugated iron to the extent that they are interchangeable'. Philip Drew, op. cit., p.64. Murcutt himself concedes only that the materials are 'not dissimilar'.

60 North in the southern hemisphere being of course equivalent to south, in the northern hemisphere.

61 As discussed, and for reasons given, earlier.

62 'It is a characteristic of the 20th century that architects are highly selective in determining which problems they want to solve. Mies, for instance, makes many wonderful buildings only because he ignores many aspects... If he solved more problems, his buildings would be far less potent.' Paul Rudolph quoted in Robert Venturi, *Complexity and Contradiction in Architecture*, Architectural Press, London, 1977, p.17. First published 1966.